S0-AYX-286

African American History
The Migration North

By James De Medeiros

Published by Weigl Publishers Inc.
350 5th Avenue, Suite 3304, PMB 6G
New York, NY 10118-0069

Website: www.weigl.com
Copyright ©2009 WEIGL PUBLISHERS INC.

Library of Congress Cataloging-in-Publication Data available upon request.
Fax 1-866-44-WEIGL for the attention of the Publishing Records department.

ISBN 978-1-59036-880-0 (hard cover)
ISBN 978-1-59036-881-7 (soft cover)

Printed in the United States of America
1 2 3 4 5 6 7 8 9 0 12 11 10 09 08

Weigl acknowledges Getty Images as its primary image supplier for this title.

Editor: Heather C. Hudak
Designer: Terry Paulhus

Contents

Moving North

The migration of African Americans from the southern states to the northern states was one of the most important developments in the history of the United States.

At its core, the migration was a protest to the conditions in the South. African Americans left the South for the North because it was the only safe way to voice their displeasure over the way they were treated following **Reconstruction**.

Slavery had ended, but **segregation** and **discrimination** persisted. Angry mobs of people of European ancestry intimidated African Americans with threats of violence that often turned to **lynching**. Laws were passed to make life in the South very difficult. The result was that African Americans began leaving the South in large numbers.

The period of the migration north lasted from 1916 until 1970. Historians have noted that this era was shaped by two major events. During the Great Depression in the 1930s, migration to the North substantially decreased. However,

People who had been slaves all their lives had a difficult time adjusting to life as free people.

with the beginning of World War II, migration continued at a greater rate than ever before.

TECHNOLOGY LINK

To find out more about the events that shaped the migration north, visit **www.jimcrowhistory. com/org/history/history.htm**.

Segregation laws extended to public transportation. African Americans could not sit in the same places as people of European ancestry.

Legal Discrimination

Before the **Civil War**, African Americans living in the South worked and lived as slaves. They often were mistreated and forced to work against their will. At the time, southerners of European ancestry were legally able to enforce slavery. With the victory of the North in the Civil War, slavery officially ended.

However, while slavery was no longer legal, the poor treatment that African Americans received continued. While African Americans were free to live and work as they pleased, this meant very little to former slave owners. These people made it very difficult for African Americans to find work or housing.

In addition, local governments tried to force African Americans to leave the South. Threats were common. Lynching, humiliation, and **intimidation** became part of southern culture.

In many states, particularly in the South, laws were put in effect that allowed for segregation in all public facilities. Often, the facilities provided for African Americans were in poor condition compared to those for people of European ancestry. These segregation laws were in full force in every southern state by the early 1900s. Races were kept separate in nearly every aspect of life.

African Americans became increasingly frustrated with their

situation. At the conclusion of the Civil War, they had expected to receive fair and equal treatment under the law, and they had been promised the right to vote. However, other southerners found ways to prevent this from happening. The only freedom that African Americans received was the ability to move around the country. Many African Americans believed that this freedom of movement was their only hope for a better life.

In the pre-Civil War days, many African Americans attempted to cross the Mason-Dixon line to escape from slavery. After Reconstruction, many freed slaves moved across this border in order to avoid the violence and limited opportunities that continued to be common in the South.

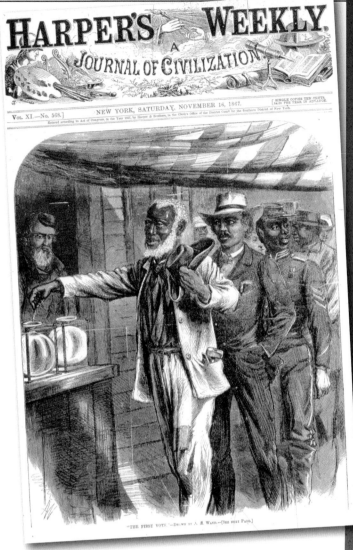

During the Reconstruction era, African American men gained the right to vote.

Quick Facts

The Mason-Dixon line was a symbolic line that separated the South from the North in the eastern part of the United States. The line was first drawn to end a dispute between British **colonies** in the mid-1760s. The states bordering the line were West Virginia, Pennsylvania, Maryland, and Delaware. Later, the line served as a cultural boundary, defining the areas directly north and south of the line.

Reconstruction took place after the Civil War, between 1865 and 1877. During this time, the northern and southern states reunited. It was a time of transition for freed slaves, former slave owners, and governments.

Time for Change

African Americans had great optimism at the end of the Civil War in 1865. The northern states had won, putting an end to slavery. Reconstruction was about to begin.

In the years that followed the war, that optimism began to fade. The war had caused enormous damage to cities, and many lives were lost. People across the country began to tire of the African American fight for equality, and the focus turned to rebuilding what they had lost during the conflict.

Efforts to control the freedom, power, and financial success of African Americans began almost immediately after the Civil War ended. Though free, African Americans in the southern states still had to live by special rules, such as curfews. Both African Americans and people of European ancestry had to adapt to the changes taking place in society. This proved to be a great challenge. It seemed the only way to improve the situation was with a mass migration of African Americans to the northern states.

Slaves would often work more than 12 hours a day on plantations.

Jim Crow South

Many southerners of European ancestry were not happy about the end of slavery. They showed their dissatisfaction through violence, and by passing laws that created segregation in the South. The Jim Crow laws were named after the song "Jump Jim Crow," which was performed by a man of European ancestry whose face was painted black to imitate an African American performer.

The **Civil Rights** Act of 1875 banned all forms of segregation in places that were freely open to all citizens. However, in 1883, the United States **Supreme Court** withdrew the ban on segregation. With that decision, the southern states were able to take away many of the freedoms that African Americans had received with their emancipation.

The Jim Crow laws gave southerners of European ancestry the ability to segregate public places such as parks, transportation, and public schools. Separate sections were reserved for African Americans in public places. Soon, **interracial** marriages were banned, and attempts were made to prevent African American males from being able to vote. The majority of these segregation laws began passing in the 1890s.

The "separate but equal" concept continued to be used until 1954.

Separate but Equal

African Americans responded to segregation in many ways. The first response came from Homer Plessy in 1892. Homer was an African American who, on a train trip through Louisiana, sat in a seat reserved for people of European ancestry. Homer was arrested, his case went to court, and he was found guilty. The court ruled that, because African Americans were given separate but equal space on the train, they did not have the right to complain about the situation.

The decision of "separate but equal" gave southerners of European ancestry the means to discriminate against African Americans. At the time, very few African Americans had received an education, and therefore many of them could not read. Most African Americans also had little money due to their years of slavery. When it came time to vote, many governments used these situations to their advantage by insisting that voters pay a tax before casting ballots. Some governments also made it mandatory for anyone wanting to vote to pass a literacy test.

By 1910, segregation laws had been passed in each of the southern states that previously made up the **Confederacy**. This meant that nearly every public place in the South, including hospitals, transportation, washrooms, and cemeteries, had designated areas for African Americans. Some states even prevented African Americans from working in the same room as people of European ancestry. It was almost impossible for the two races to come together in any way.

Despite these challenges, African Americans had gained two key freedoms as a result of the Civil War. They now had the ability to freely move around the country as well as to gather with fellow African Americans. The African American community took full advantage of these opportunities and created their own culture within the country.

As they struggled to make the transition from slavery to freedom, African Americans were required to work in the agricultural industry only. It was similar to their former work, though they had to provide their own homes and food. Farm owners paid a share of the crop they cultivated, and owned all the products they grew. This meant that African Americans remained poor and reliant on the farm owner. This made it almost impossible for African Americans to financially succeed the same way as people of European ancestry.

After fighting for freedom, this was a tough reality to accept. Many African Americans chose to dream of a better land where they would be given some opportunities to succeed. Many of those people went north.

Once freed, African Americans were only allowed to hold jobs on farms, or as housekeepers.

Ku Klux Klan

The Reconstruction era saw the rise of a group known as the Ku Klux Klan (KKK). Founded in 1866, the KKK strongly opposed African Americans receiving any rights. It was the group's goal to take away the rights African Americans received after the Civil War, as well as to strip them of all opportunities.

Recruitment to the KKK was especially easy in the former Confederate states. Many people of European ancestry saw the KKK as a way to rule the South through violence and intimidation. One of their first acts of aggression was against the **Republican** leaders they blamed for freeing African American slaves.

Though the Civil Rights Act of 1871 limited the ability of the KKK to act against African Americans, the Jim Crow laws opened doors for the KKK to legally commit acts of violence. The Ku Klux Klan used intimidation as their primary weapon. This came in the form of burning crosses, beatings, lynchings, and killings. African American symbols of accomplishment,

The first slaves who saw members of the KKK wearing their traditional white robes thought they were seeing the ghosts of Confederate soldiers.

including churches, schools, and businesses, were destroyed. Successful African Americans were more likely to be targeted by the group. However, regardless of their achievements, African Americans often were terrorized as part of their every day lives. The brutality was considered acceptable, and as a result, many of these acts were not recorded in history.

The Ku Klux Klan's activities were a factor in driving out many African Americans from the South. Many African Americans felt they would not be safe unless they left.

In 1915, the film *The Birth of a Nation* helped revive the Ku Klux Klan on a national level, with a stronger urban presence. The KKK were concerned about the establishment of the **National Association for the Advancement of Colored People** (NAACP) and African American demands for full citizenship within the United States. The KKK opposed African American rights, as well as the changing role of women in society. They wanted to return to pre-Civil War values—a time when southern people of European ancestry held power over everything and opportunities were not extended to others.

The Birth of a Nation

*T*he *Birth of a Nation* made the KKK appear as though they were the heroes of the Reconstruction era. The movie was based on Thomas Dixon's play *The Clansman*. It begins with a look at pre-Civil War life and ends with the Reconstruction era and the Ku Klux Klan's attempt to restore the South to its former situation. The movie was highly controversial, and African Americans protested it in most cities where it played. Many major cities refused to allow the film to be shown.

Lynching

Following the end of the Civil War, lynching was one way that southerners of European ancestry attempted to stay in control of the South. While the definition of lynching changed over time, it generally included such things as murders by way of hanging or burning, as well as humiliation. Most lynching victims were African Americans.

The NAACP, the Tuskegee Normal and Industrial Institute, and other organizations kept records about lynchings once these acts became common in the 1880s. These groups found that most lynchings occurred in the South. However, at least one-fifth of these acts took place in the northern states. Texas, Georgia, and Mississippi had the highest number of victims.

Those African Americans who escaped lynching were still exposed to it in some way. Lynchings often

In the 1930s, an anti-lynching bill was drafted. Texas senator Tom Connally opposed the bill.

were public displays, and mobs forced African Americans to watch while another African American was lynched. In some places, such as Birmingham, Kentucky, warning notices were posted to indicate that any African Americans should leave or become victims themselves.

Lynchings likely played a role in the northern migration of many African Americans. In the hostile environment that lynchings created, many African Americans feared for their lives. They were intimidated by large mobs of people that threatened them.

Some African Americans felt as though they had no choice but to migrate north. African Americans fled the South in record numbers, leaving behind many of their personal possessions.

The NAACP campaigned for new members in an effort to promote civil rights and equality for all U.S. citizens.

The NAACP led peaceful marches to protest the lynching of African Americans.

Quick Facts

The term "lynching" may date back to the late eighteenth century when Virginia justice of the peace Charles Lynch used violent means to punish people he felt were taking part in a **Loyalist** uprising.

Lynching decreased in the decades following Reconstruction. However, it increased as the country entered the twentieth century.

Sometimes, people of European ancestry were lynching victims, especially if they were suspected of helping African Americans.

Booker T. Washington

Booker T. Washington was born a slave in Hale's Ford, Virginia, on April 5, 1856. He was the son of an African American slave named Jane. His father, was a man of European ancestry from a nearby farm.

After gaining his freedom, Washington worked in many labor jobs before attending the Hampton Institute, and later Wayland Seminary. After graduation, Washington worked as a teacher at Hampton Institute before taking a position at the Tuskegee Normal and Industrial Institute in Alabama. Washington was just 25 years old when he became principal of the school. A strong believer in self-reliance, Washington had students carry out housekeeping and agricultural tasks at the school. Students also helped construct the buildings of the institute.

As an educator, leader, and advocate for African American civil rights, Washington believed that African Americans should be more conservative in their approach to gaining equality. He thought that African Americans should not fight to gain equal rights with people of European ancestry. Washington felt that it was best for African Americans to concentrate on improving their economic situation and the quality of their characters. This way, Americans of European ancestry would come to live peacefully and respectfully with African Americans. Many politicians and people in the United States supported his views.

In addition to his work as an educator, Washington was a gifted speaker who made presentations on behalf of African American rights. He received many honorary degrees for his work.

Washington influenced many newspapers with this ideas and also helped some of them financially. Other newspapers were strongly against his ideas.

Washington died of heart failure at 59 years of age.

Members of the Republican party consulted with Booker T. Washington on national issues.

African American Publications

At the end of the Civil War, the newspaper became the voice of free African Americans. Literacy rates were improving, so African Americans used the power of the press to continue their fight for equality. In 1829, *Freedom's Journal* was the first African American newspaper to write about the African American community. It was the start of a new era in publishing. By the early 1900s, hundreds of publications catered to African Americans. Yet, these publications upset southerners of European ancestry. Their anger led to attacks against anyone associated with one of these publications.

Many weekly newspapers wrote about the freedom and liberty available in the northern states. In this way, African American newspapers contributed to the migration of African Americans to the northern states.

Northern newspapers became the choice of most African Americans. They could more freely explain to readers the events that were taking place in the country, and in particular, the South.

In 1905, the newspaper the *Chicago Defender* was first published. In the beginning, it supported Booker's

to stress that African Americans should move north. At this time, Chicago had a need for workers. The newspaper promoted the city as a land of opportunities. It made the point that the South was violent and anti-African American.

By 1919, nearly two-thirds of the *Chicago Defender*'s readers lived in the south. The newspaper captivated African American and motivated them into action. The result was massive growth in the African American population of Chicago.

The *Chicago Defender* catered to African American readers.

Other newspapers across the North had similar success, including the *Baltimore Afro-American* and the *Pittsburgh Courier*. Like the *Chicago Defender*, these newspapers focused on successful African Americans , such as including Langston Hughes and W.E.B. Du Bois.

In 1932, the *Baltimore Afro-American* announced its support for **Democratic** presidential candidate Franklin Delano Roosevelt in the upcoming election. At the time, most African Americans voted Republican. The influence of the African American press was demonstrated when when Franklin Roosevelt won the election.

Newspapers, such as the *Chicago Defender*, were a source of pride for the African American community.

Marcus Mosiah Garvey

After traveling around the world, in 1914, Marcus Mosiah Garvey returned to his home in St. Ann's Bay, Jamaica, and started the African Communities League and Universal Negro Improvement and Conservation Association. The organization sought to unite African Americans around the world in a quest for better rights.

Two years later, Garvey moved to the United States, where he quickly established a following. In 1917, he founded the Universal Negro Improvement Association (UNIA), in Harlem, New York. This new organization focused on helping African Americans fight against lynchings and the Jim Crow laws. Garvey encouraged segregation and believed that African Americans would never find equal treatment in the United States. He felt they should move back to Africa. To express his ideas, Garvey began publishing the newspaper *Negro World* in 1919. By this time, the UNIA had more than two million members.

Garvey was known for having many ideas about the best way for African Americans to secure a better future. One of his ideas was a plan to establish the Negro Factories Corporation in major cities in the United States and other parts of the world. This company included laundries, grocery stores, restaurants, a publishing house, and clothing factories that were operated by African Americans. Garvey also launched the Black Star Line, a fleet of steamships intended to carry African American people and goods to Africa.

In August 1920, Garvey brought Africans from all over the world to New York City to discuss issues that affected all of them. Following the **convention**, Garvey called for

Marcus Garvey shared his opinions about slavery, saying, "For man to know himself is for him to feel that for him there is no human master."

a new declaration of rights for all Africans around the world.

Garvey helped create a sense of nationalism among African Americans. With the migration north in full force after World War I, many believed that change would happen if they followed Garvey's advice.

By 1922, the UNIA started having financial troubles. When Garvey decided to meet with a member of the Ku Klux Klan, it cemented the end of the organization. Garvey was no longer viewed as a great leader, and UNIA membership began to decline. Many respected members, including African American civil rights **activist** W.E.B. Du Bois, left the organization. Garvey was charged in 1923 with **mail fraud** and later deported to Jamaica.

Despite this, Garvey is considered one of the most influential forces on African American culture during the 1920s. He helped bring out the pride and identity that African Americans had been seeking.

Marcus Garvey had many dedicated followers.

Negro World

Marcus Garvey established *Negro World* newspaper in 1918 and continued to publish it until 1933. It was used as the voice of Garvey's Universal Negro Improvement and Conservation Association and stressed the concepts of self-help and economic independence.

In the weekly newspaper, readers were treated to African history and poetry, as well as editorials written by Garvey. While it was banned in some parts of the world, the New York based publication became so popular that copies of it would be smuggled globally. With its global presence also came the introduction of French and Spanish language editions.

The Work of the NAACP

The National Association for the Advancement of Colored People (NAACP) was founded on February 12, 1909, by a group of African American civil rights activists and a few people of European ancestry. Its purpose was to work on gaining full civil rights for African Americans.

In 1908, a race **riot** broke out in Springfield, Illinois, at a time when African Americans were beginning to migrate to the area at a steady pace. Two African Americans were arrested, but many citizens of European ancestry wanted more action to be taken. They attacked African Americans, killing at least seven people.

Fearing the violence would continue, a small group of people of European ancestry and African

Americans met in New York City to discuss human rights and equality, including the right to vote. This group became known as the NAACP. At first, people of European ancestry dominated leadership positions within the group. However, African American member W.E.B. Du Bois was instrumental in shaping the framework for the goals of the organization.

Branches were quickly set up in Boston, Philadelphia, Chicago, and Washington, DC. When a major incident of violence or discrimination occurred, another branch was formed in that area. There were 71 branches of the NAACP by 1916, but only three of these were located in the southern states. That soon changed. The

The NAACP displayed a black flag from their office window in New York to mark each lynching.

NAACP refused to be intimidated by the Ku Klux Klan. In 1920, the NAACP held its annual conference in Atlanta, Georgia, which was considered one of the KKK's most active areas. By this time, there were more than 300 NAACP branches, with over 130 located in the South. Membership in the NAACP continued to grow as African Americans migrated north.

Even though African Americans were leaving oppression in the South, they still faced discrimination in the North. The NAACP worked to correct this. However, race riots began breaking out in the North, while the South continued to be terrorized by lynchings. The NAACP worked hard at introducing anti-lynching legislation, while also tackling the issues of residential and school segregation faced by African Americans.

The issue of school segregation showcased the determination of the NAACP to gain equal rights. African Americans born in the North wanted to end school segregation. Meanwhile, those who had just moved from the South favored school segregation because they worried their children would receive poor treatment from teachers of European ancestry. African American teachers also embraced segregation, as they did not have the opportunity to teach at schools for children of European ancestry. The NAACP, however, continued to fight for the end of school segregation in the name of equality.

W.E.B. Du Bois

Born in Great Barrington, Massachusetts, on February 23, 1868, William Edward Burghardt Du Bois was a well-known African American scholar, historian, **sociologist**, and activist. Du Bois. was dedicated to the fight for civil rights, and he helped African Americans distance themselves from the "Uncle Tom" image.

Being from the North, Du Bois had not been subject to the type of racism that African Americans living in the South faced. His introduction to the true difficulties imposed by racism came when he attended Fisk College in Nashville, Tennessee, in the late 1880s. Many of Du Bois' ideas about civil rights and gaining full freedom for his race began to form while he attended Fisk College.

Upon graduating from Fisk, Du Bois attended Harvard University, earning a master's degree in 1891. He then worked on a doctorate degree at the University of Berlin in Germany before returning to Harvard to complete the degree. Du Bois' studies in Germany helped him understand that racial issues existed in other parts of the world as well. He began to view the problems of African Americans as a global issue affecting the entire race.

After completing his studies, Du Bois worked as a teacher in Wilberforce, Ohio, for a few years. In 1896, he accepted a University

In 1961, the President of Ghana invited Du Bois to direct the Encyclopedia Africana. Two years later, the U.S. refused to give Du Bois a new passport, and he became a citizen of Ghana.

of Pennsylvania fellowship that extended the opportunity to study African Americans living in Philadelphia's underprivileged communities.

In 1903, Du Bois published his first book, *The Souls of Black Folk*. In the book, Du Bois discusses the African American identity and the ideas of Booker T. Washington.

In all of his books, Du Bois shared his belief that Africans, as a **global community**, needed to educate themselves and learn about their history and culture in order to gain equality. This vision was instrumental in the early development of the NAACP. However, Du Bois later resigned from the NAACP, believing that it was more important to receive equal funding for separate African American schools than it was to end the segregated school system. This focus on educating African Americans about their culture was a key factor in prompting Du Bois to lead a pan-African congress discussion about important issues facing all Africans around the world.

Uncle Tom

Uncle Tom was a character in Harriet Beecher Stowe's 1852 anti-slavery novel *Uncle Tom's Cabin*. Stowe was a woman of European ancestry who opposed slavery and helped slaves escape. She wanted to write a novel with an obvious anti-slavery message, and the result was *Uncle Tom's Cabin*.

The lead character in the book was inspired by the real-life stories of Reverend Josiah Henson. Josiah spent 30 years as a slave on a plantation in Montgomery County, Maryland, before he escaped in 1819. After his escape, Josiah became a Methodist preacher, abolitionist, lecturer, and founder of a colony of former slaves in Canada.

Later, the term "Uncle Tom" became used to describe African Americans who were thought to be overly accommodating to all ideas of people of European ancestry.

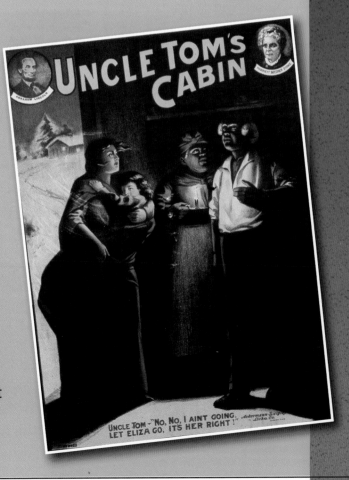

Chicago: The Top Destination

In 1910, African Americans only accounted for about two percent of Chicago's population. The city was known for its manufacturing, steel mills, and packing houses. When tensions started to mount in Europe, and World War I began, European **immigrants** stopped moving to Chicago. There was a great void to fill, which created many employment opportunities for African Americans. Companies that had previously been unwilling to hire African Americans began to actively recruit them from the South. African Americans began migrating to Chicago in large numbers, making Chicago the top destination for African Americans who were looking to leave the South.

At one point during the migration north, 3,000 African Americans were arriving every week in Chicago.

Between 1916 and 1919, more than 50,000 African Americans migrated to Chicago from the South. It was a good situation for companies looking to keep up with production needs, as well as for African Americans in search of a better life. The *Chicago Defender* was heavily involved in this process. The newspaper had become very popular in the southern states and would routinely run features detailing the violence in the South alongside job opportunities in Chicago. Chicago's higher wages and greater freedom were also reported.

Between 1940 and 1960, the population of the South Side of Chicago increased 77 percent.

Some migrants moved to Chicago to establish roots so that friends and family from the southern states would have a place to live when they migrated. Others, moved to Chicago to rejoin family or friends. New **networks** were being formed continuously. Over time, most African Americans knew someone who had made the trip. They could depend on this person to help them leave the South. For those who needed help adjusting to life in the North, the Chicago Urban League was formed in 1916. This group helped African Americans find work and places to live in the city.

TECHNOLOGY LINK
To find out more about the Chicago Urban League, visit **www.thechicagourban league.org.**

Race Riots

Most African Americans lived in Chicago's South Side. The population in that area had a greater number African Americans than people of European ancestry. This gave most migrants the feeling that they belonged in a free and welcoming environment. However, one of the main reasons that African Americans lived in this area was because housing discrimination left them with little choice.

African Americans may have been migrating to Chicago for a better life, but many people of European ancestry did not share their enthusiasm. Discrimination was still a factor. Some people used intimidation tactics to make certain that African Americans would stay out of their neighborhoods.

Tensions mounted, and in July 1919, a race riot broke out. A young African American man inadvertently swam into a part of a beach that was mainly used by people of European ancestry. He drowned after being struck in the head by a rock that had been thrown by a person of European ancestry. For two weeks, angry mobs of African Americans and people of European ancestry clashed with one another in fighting across the city's South Side. On the fourth day of rioting, the government sent the state **militia** to restore order, but the fighting continued. In the end, the riots claimed the lives of 38 Chicagoans—23 African Americans and 15 people of European ancestry. In addition, more than 500 people were injured, and hundreds of

During the summer of 1919, race riots erupted in as many as 20 American cities. The largest and most violent of these riots took place in Chicago.

families lost everything when their homes were set on fire by rioters.

The Second Wave of Migrants

When the Great Depression started in 1929, it affected the entire country. During the 1930s, fewer African Americans migrated to Chicago. When the need for industrial labor and cotton production became important issues at the beginning of World War II, African Americans once again began migrating to Chicago.

Many new positions opened between 1940 and 1944, as people left to join the war effort overseas. This wave of migration was even larger than the first. Between 1940 and 1970, about three times as many African Americans migrated to Chicago than during the previous period of migration.

Again, most African Americans moved to Chicago's South Side. This time, they also began moving into the West Side as well. However, many people of European ancestry still discriminated against them. Tensions once again mounted, as people of European ancestry sought ways to keep African Americans from moving in to other parts of Chicago.

By 1970, more than 500,000 African Americans had migrated from the southern states to Chicago. African Americans looked for help in their battle against discrimination and segregation. Help came in the form of Martin Luther King, Jr.

Martin Luther King, Jr.

Martin Luther King, Jr. was born in Atlanta, Georgia, in 1929. At age 15, he attended Morehouse College. After college, King attended Crozier Theological Seminary in Pennsylvania, where he studied to become a minister. Before accepting a position at the Dexter Avenue Baptist Church, King completed his doctorate degree at Boston University in 1954. As a minister and community leader, King had a great influence on the Civil Rights Movement. He was a gifted speaker, and his message of nonviolence inspired people to take action.

At the height of the Civil Rights Movement, between 1957 and 1968, King traveled more

than 6 million miles across the country, making more than 2,500 public appearances. He participated in protests and wrote articles and books to educate people about the injustices African Americans faced.

Harlem: A Place for a Renaissance

Chicago may have been the city that most migrants flocked to, but many African Americans also moved to Harlem, New York. Like Chicago, Harlem offered greater opportunities and freedom. Harlem would shape African American history with its contributions in the form of riots and writing

In addition to being a land of opportunity for migrants, many African American contributions to the arts and, in particular, literature, came from people who lived there. For nearly two decades following the release of W.E.B. Du Bois' *The Souls of Black Folk* in 1903, few African American books were published

In 1965, civil rights activists in Harlem marched in protest of violent acts taking place in Alabama.

In 1922, *Harlem Shadows* by Claude McKay sparked a new interest in the field. This interest become known as the "Harlem **Renaissance**," and it lasted throughout the 1920s and into the 1930s. One of the most important books written during the era was *The New Negro*.

The New Negro portrayed African Americans as strong, independent people who would no longer play the "Uncle Tom" role of accommodating the ideas of people of European ancestry. By the 1930s, the Renaissance era ended. Few of the writers had been migrants, and their writing did not captivate southern African Americans. As well, the Great Depression changed the economy.

During the Great Depression, unemployment rates climbed to new levels. About half of Harlem's African Americans were left jobless during this period. In 1935, a riot broke out after a 16-year-old African American was jailed for stealing from a Harlem department store. Even though he was released, a mob gathered on 125th Street and caused about $2 million in property damage. The two-day riot resulted in two deaths. Local authorities determined that the riot was caused in part by economic times, and also because of racial injustices. Services for African Americans improved, including the opening of the country's first federally **subsidized** housing project called the Harlem River Houses.

On August 1, 1943, another riot erupted when an African American soldier knocked down a police officer who was of European ancestry. The officer responded by shooting soldier. Rumors circulated that the soldier died. Property damage, violence, and **looting** followed. In the end, six people died. This event demonstrated African American frustration at racial injustice.

Discrimination in Workplaces

Migrants leaving the South sought more freedom and employment opportunities in the North. While the situation in the North was an improvement over the conditions in the South, migrants still faced discrimination.

Northern employers and co-workers of European ancestry often treated African Americans poorly, including segregating African Americans from the rest of the workforce. They faced restrictions and inequalities that included being placed in more dangerous positions and receiving fewer chances at advancement.

Most African Americans received significantly lower wages than people of European ancestry who were doing the same work. Sometimes, this was the result of the fact that many African Americans lacked a proper education—not having had the opportunity to learn as slaves. Similarly, discrimination in the workplace made it difficult for African Americans to upgrade their education.

Competition existed among people of European ancestry and African Americans for jobs that required little training. This competition led many African Americans to try to seek help from **unions**. However,

African American singer Marian Anderson performed in Washington, DC, in 1939, after she was barred from singing at two other venues because of her race.

few workplace unions helped prevent discrimination. Some unions would not grant membership to African Americans, and others kept African Americans from working in certain industries. On the other hand, unions such as the Congress of Industrial Organizations believed it was their duty to make the workplace situation better for all employees, regardless of race.

By the 1930s, the Congress of Industrial Organization had implemented anti-discrimination policies and worked hard to correct the concerns that existed in industries that hired African Americans. This gave African Americans the opportunity to compete fairly with people of European ancestry.

However, racial stereotypes continued to grow in other lines of work. This prevented African Americans from receiving equal opportunities elsewhere.

Quick Facts

There was an unspoken and unwritten rule that African Americans were never to be placed in positions of power over people of European ancestry.

In most cases, the only time an African American would be given a position in management was if the workers being managed were also African Americans.

As a result of slavery, African Americans were thought to be best employed in positions that involved physical labor.

A New Home for Migrants

When African Americans migrated north, finding a place to live became a major challenge. Due to economic conditions and racism, they had little choice but to find housing in ghettos. Ghettos are residential areas dominated by particular cultural groups. These areas are usually in the oldest and most worn-down parts of a city's downtown area.

For many African Americans at the time, housing was not their main concern. They were willing to maintain a level of segregation in order to escape harsh living conditions in the South.

People of European ancestry worked hard to keep African Americans from entering their communities. Real estate agents, landowners, and banks did their best to steer African Americans to ghettos. They also ensured that properties in areas where people of European ancestry lived never became available options for African Americans to buy or rent. In rare instances when African Americans were able to move into these areas, they often did not stay for long. Violence and intimidation forced them to reconsider their move.

By the end of the 1920s, Harlem, New York, was home to the largest number of African-American migrants in the United States.

Ghettos had poor quality housing, but the cost of renting or purchasing in other areas was extremely high. With African Americans receiving low wages, it was nearly impossible for them to rise above their conditions to live in better communities. Instead, most African Americans tried to make the best of their situation. They used their freedom to create an enjoyable atmosphere that was filled with family and friends.

In the 1930s, ghettos gained popularity in many major cities in the northern states. Following World War II, African American populations began to grow at a rapid pace, and the growth made it more difficult to find affordable housing. Urban redevelopment became a major problem for many cities. In some places, houses were torn down, regardless of their quality, as a means to remove African Americans from parts of the city.

Quick Facts

African American migration into ghettos was one of the main reasons riots that broke out in at least 20 cities throughout the United States in 1919.

New York City, Chicago, and Philadelphia were the sites of the first ghettos in the United States prior to World War I.

During the late 1960s, frustration from living in the ghettos led to riots in Los Angeles, Cleveland, and Detroit.

Throughout cities across the United States, segregation of African Americans continued to rise until it reached its peak in the 1960s.

Military Service and the World Wars

Military service likely was one of the main reasons for the early stages of the migration north. For many African Americans who fought in World War I, it was their first time leaving the South. In spite of the physically demanding and dangerous circumstances, many African Americans were impressed with how they were treated in the North as well as in France. The freedom that many African Americans found in the North caused them to want to move there when World War I ended.

Many African Americans still experienced racism during and after World War I. Segregated units were used to ensure limited interaction between races. Upon returning home to the southern states, African Americans were targeted by people of European ancestry who did not want them to have equal rights, even after their time in the army. The violence and anger directed at African Americans became the last straw for many, who quickly decided to leave the South and move north.

World War II would prove to be another major cause of migration. By serving in the military, African Americans realized the opportunity to learn new job skills and receive equal pay. The Selective Service Act of 1940 helped break down barriers because, for the first time ever, African Americans were

During World War I, the African American unit the 369th were awarded the French medal the Croix de Guerre for bravery in battle.

The navy was racially segregated until the United States entered World War II.

able to serve in both the army and navy. This meant they could train to become pilots and mechanics, or learn other job skills that would greatly help them at the conclusion of the war.

Of the more than one million African American men and women serving their country, most were in the **infantry**. They had little choice, as the navy continued to impose restrictions on the types of positions African Americans could fill, and the marines only started recruiting African Americans in 1942. African American newspapers began to report on discrimination within the armed forces and focused on the contributions and successes of African American soldiers.

This four-year effort to end discrimination became known as the "Double V Campaign."

Launched by the *Pittsburgh Courier*, an African American newspaper, the term "Double V" symbolized a double victory over both the **fascism** that existed internationally and racism that existed in the United States. A "Double V" logo was featured on the cover page of every edition of the newspaper to raise awareness of these issues. The campaign gained widespread appeal and forced President Roosevelt to notice the racial issues within the military. The armed forces became the first American institution to desegregate.

African Americans risked losing their jobs, their homes, or even their lives if they challenged the Jim Crow laws, such as drinking from a water fountain meant for people of European ancestry.

Early Stages of the Civil Rights Movement

Migrants leaving their homes in the South were doing so as a means of protesting living conditions. In the Jim Crow south, there was poor education, violent discrimination, and a lack of equality and freedom. Even the right to vote was made difficult for African Americans. The North promised greater freedom and more workplace opportunities, but there still was not true equality. Equality would

only be gained through the Civil Rights Movement.

Some of the most visible gains in the early stages of the Civil Rights Movement included the "Double V" campaign. African Americans wanted to use World War II as their opportunity to prove that they should be treated as equals. However, they had to put pressure on the government to provide this opportunity. Discrimination made it

African American students had to work hard to gain the respect of students of European ancestry.

joined with others to fight for their rights. With migration, membership in the NAACP continued to increased.

The fight for civil rights was both violent and peaceful. Many times, African Americans held demonstrations, **boycotts**, and **sit-ins**, with the idea to create change. Sometimes, their protests were met with a violent response.

As a result of the migration, the African American population became grew very large in the northern states. Over time, these huge populations influenced politics, allowing for some changes to take place. However, these changes happened slowly.

In 1954, the *Brown v. Board of Education* ruling ended school segregation. In spite of some successes, other changes would continue to be very difficult.

difficult for African Americans to be given responsibility and fair treatment in the armed forces. African Americans won this battle, and anti-discrimination laws forced greater equality in the armed forces.

The Civil Rights Movement spanned decades. In many ways, it began with the migration north. Once in their newfound northern homes, southern African Americans

Brown v. Board of Education

One of the hundreds of cases filed by the NAACP was *Brown v. The Board of Education of Topeka*. The case was filed on behalf of Linda Brown, a 17-year-old student who was not allowed to attend her local high school because she was African American.

Civil rights lawyers argued that schools had rarely, if ever, been equal. On May 17, 1954, the court handed down a unanimous decision stating that "separate educational facilities are inherently unequal." As a result, racial segregation was ruled a violation of the Fourteenth Amendment of the United States Constitution.

The ruling angered some people, and many southern states opposed the Supreme Court's judgment. In response, some communities closed their public schools and opened private schools that only students of European ancestry could attend.

A Victory in the Fight for Rights

African Americans activists, many of whom organized themselves at churches, continued to press for civil rights into the 1960s. Martin Luther King, Jr. would eventually step forward to lead the cause. With his incredible skills as a public speaker, he was able to make the American population understand why discrimination should be

In May 1954, the United States Supreme Court ruled segregated education unconstitutional. The court gave schools one year to comply with the ruling.

stopped and civil rights should be granted. The movement gained momentum, and many people of European ancestry began to support the African American cause. In 1964, the fight for civil rights and equality was rewarded with the passing of Civil Rights Act. This landmark act was a piece of legislation that outlawed segregation in schools, public places, and employment.

When African Americans were enslaved, they did their best to escape and try to help those left behind. When discrimination took the place of slavery in the South, African Americans left the South as a way to protect themselves and protest their living conditions. Again, those who left helped others also leave the South. The North offered a safer place to live, as well as more freedom and opportunity. However, it still did not offer African Americans their civil rights. They took a stand and were finally granted their civil rights. With these rights, African American success stories have become more common.

In the era of the Jim Crow south, African Americans received poor education opportunities. Today,

Throughout the twentieth century new opportunities became available for African Americans. In 1963, Sidney Poitier became the first African American to win an Academy Award for Best Actor.

African Americans receive the same education as people of European ancestry. They can attend college and work in any profession they choose, such as medicine, law, and science. Their incredible successes are evident in all areas, including sports, arts, and entertainment.

TECHNOLOGY LINK
To learn more about African Americans' fight for equality, visit **www.naacp.org**.

Timeline

1619: Africans are captured and brought to Jamestown, Virginia, to work as slaves.

1619

1865: Congress passes the Thirteenth Amendment, which outlaws slavery.

1866: Congress passes the Civil Rights Act, which declares African Americans as citizens.

1861

1807: Congress declares it illegal to bring slaves into the United States.

1831-1861: About 75,000 slaves escape by the Underground Railroad, a network that helped protect and hide escaped slaves so they could find freedom.

1861: The Civil War begins. One of the main issues behind the conflict is to determine if slavery should be allowed.

1909

1863: President Abraham Lincoln passes the Emancipation Proclamation, which legally frees all slaves.

1881: The first Jim Crow Law is passed in Tennessee.

1896: In Plessy v. Ferguson, the Supreme Court rules that public places may be segregated as long as equal facilities are given to African Americans.

1909: The National Association for the Advancement of Colored People (NAACP) is formed.

1910-1920: During a period known as the Great Migration, about 500,000 African Americans move to northern states.

1914: Marcus Garvey forms the Universal Negro Improvement Association in Jamaica. The group eventually opens branches in the United States.

1919: A series of violent events occur in response to the Great Migration. The period is known as "Red Summer" because of the hundreds of deaths that resulted from the violence.

1600   **1800**   **1850**   **1900**

1942: The Congress of Racial Equality (CORE) is started in Chicago.

1948: President Truman desegregates the army.

1954: In Brown v. Board of Education of Topeka, the Supreme Court rules against school segregation.

1955: The Montgomery Bus Boycott begins when Rosa Parks refuses to give up her seat to a passenger of European ancestry.

1957: A community in Little Rock, Arkansas opposes desegregation and plans a protest to prevent nine African American students from entering a school that was formerly for students of European ancestry. The African American students are later called "The Little Rock Nine."

1960: At a Woolworth's lunch counter in Greensboro, North Carolina, four African American college students hold the first sit-in.

1961: The Congress of Racial Equality (CORE) begins to organize Freedom Rides.

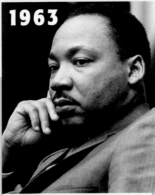
1963

1963: Martin Luther King, Jr. writes "Letter from a Birmingham Jail."

1964: Martin Luther King, Jr. is awarded the Nobel Peace Prize.

1965: Malcolm X is assassinated in New York.

1983: Astronaut Guion "Guy" S. Bluford, Jr., becomes the first African American in space, flying aboard the space shuttle *Challenger*.

1985: Philadelphia State Police bomb a house in Philadelphia occupied by an African American activist organization, MOVE, killing 11 occupants and triggering a fire that destroyed a neighborhood and left more than 300 people homeless.

1986: Martin Luther King, Jr.'s birthday is made into a national holiday.

1989: General Colin L. Powell is the first African American to be named chair of the Joint Chiefs of Staff of the U.S. military.

1989: Oprah Winfrey becomes the first African American woman to host a nationally syndicated talk show.

2008: Barack Obama, a politician from Chicago's South Side, becomes the first African American to secure a major party nomination as a presidential candidate.

1961

2008

1950   1960   1980   2000

Activity

Creating a Network

In most cases, when an African American left the South during the Great Migration, he or she would leave behind many family and friends. Over time, however, migrants became part of a growing network of people that helped other African Americans leave the South.

Everyone has many friends and family in their social network. However, sometimes these people live in other parts of the city or town, state, country, or even the world. These networks can be maintained through emails, letters, visits, and phone conversations. With the Internet, networks have the potential to grow at a rapid pace, as people are able to interact with others living at a great distance for little cost.

You will need:

✓ a pen
✓ paper
✓ a map
✓ access
  to the
  Internet

Think about the people in your network who live outside your neighborhood. They may be family, friends, people you have never met, or people you know through others.

Write a list of these people, and be sure to include the city, state, and country in which they live. Which city has the greatest number of people in your network? Locate this city on a map, and research some of its main features. Why do you think so many people you know live there?

Test Your Knowledge

Q Which states are on the border of the Mason-Dixon Line?

A West Virginia, Pennsylvania, Maryland, and Delaware

Q What does NAACP stand for?

A National Association for the Advancement of Colored People

Q Who was "Uncle Tom?"

A a character in Harriet Beecher Stowe's 1852 anti-slavery novel, Uncle Tom's Cabin.

Q Where were the first ghettos in the United States?

A New York City, Chicago, and Philadelphia

Q In which state was Homer Plessy arrested for sitting in a train seat for people of European ancestry? What year did this happen?

A in Louisiana in 1892

Q Where was Booker T. Washington born?

A Hale's Ford, Virginia

Books

Learn more about the migration north by reading the following books.

Cooper, Michael L. *Bound For the Promised Land: The Great Black Migration*. Dutton Juvenile, 1995.

Isserman, Maurice. *Journey To Freedom: The African-American Great Migration*. Facts on File, 1997.

Websites

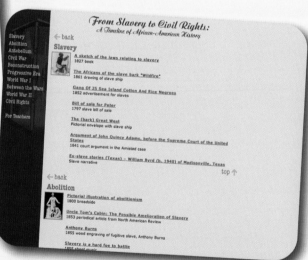

To learn more about African American history and culture, visit **www.lcweb.loc.gov/exhibits/african/intro.html**.

For more information regarding major events in African American history, visit **http://memory.loc.gov/learn/features/civilrights/learn_more.html#Top**.

Glossary

activist: a person who tries to make changes to better the circumstances of a particular cause

boycotts: protesting by refusing to use particular goods or services

civil rights: basic rights that are guaranteed to citizens of a country

Civil War: a war that took place in the United States between 1861 and 1865; states in the North and states in the South fought over the right to own slaves

colonies: groups of individuals having similar interests and occupations usually living in the same location

Confederacy: the name of the southern states during the Civil War

convention: a formal gathering to discuss issues of importance for all of those in attendance

Democratic: one of the two main political parties in the United States that arose in the 1820s

discrimination: unfair treatment due to prejudice

fascism: an extremely right-wing government that is often led by a dictator

global community: a group of people who live all over the world and share common interests

immigrants: people who move from one country to live in another

infantry: soldiers marching as a group on foot

interracial: involving different races

looting: stealing during a time of riots

Loyalist: a person who remained loyal to the British during and after the American Revolution

lynching: to kill a person without legal authority, especially by hanging

mail fraud: use of the mail system to cheat someone of money

militia: an army composed of ordinary citizens rather than professional soldiers

National Association for the Advancement of Colored People: an interracial organization working for political and civil equality of African Americans

networks: interconnected groups of people

Reconstruction: the period between 1865 and 1877 when southern states tried to rebuild and adapt to the laws of the United States

renaissance: a revival or rebirth

Republican: one of the two main political parties in the United States that arose in the 1820s

riot: a violent outbreak by a large group of people

segregation: a forced separation of races

sit-ins: organized protests in which protesters sit in one spot and refuse to move

sociologist: someone who studies the behavior of human beings

subsidized: assisted financially

Supreme Court: the highest court in the United States

unions: organizations of workers

Index

Birth of a Nation, The 13
Black Star Line 20
Brown v. Board of Education
    39, 43

Chicago 18, 22, 26, 27, 28,
    29, 30, 35, 43, 45
Chicago Defender 18, 19, 27
Chicago Urban League 27
Civil Rights Act of 1875 9, 12,
    41, 42

Double V Campaign 37
Du Bois, W.E.B. 19, 21, 22, 23,
    24, 30

Freedom's Journal 18

Garvey, Marcus 20, 21, 42
Great Depression 5, 29, 31

Harlem 20, 30, 31, 34
Harlem River Houses 31
Hughes, Langston 19

King, Martin Luther, Jr. 29,
    40, 43
Ku Klux Klan 12, 13, 21, 23

McKay, Claude 31

National Association for the
    Advancement of Colored
    People (NAACP) 13, 14,
    15, 22, 23, 25, 39, 42, 45

Plessy, Homer 10, 42, 45
Pittsburgh Courier 19, 37

Roosevelt, Franklin Delano
    19, 37

Selective Service Act
    of 1940 36
Supreme Court 9, 39, 40,
    42, 43

Universal Negro Improvement
    Association (UNIA) 20, 21

Washington, Booker T. 17,
    25, 45
World War I 26, 35, 36
World War II 5, 29, 35, 36,
    37, 38